Kami Koala
Makes A Decision

written by **Teydon Rae**

illustrated by **Cennet Kapkac**

All Rights Reserved
Copyright © 2022 by Teydon Rae
No part of this book may be reproduced or transmitted, downloaded, distributed, reversed engineered, or stored in or introduced into any information storage and retrieval system, in any form or by any means, including photocopying and recording, whether electronic or mechanical, now known or hereinafter invented without permission in writing from the publisher.

Publisher's Cataloging-in-Publication data

Names: Rae, Teydon, author. | Kapkac, Cennet, illustrator.
Title: Kami Koala makes a decision : a decision making book for kids ages 4-8 / written by Teydon Rae; illustrated by Cennet Kapkac.
Description: Snowflake, AZ: Sunny G Publishing, 2022. | Summary: Kami Koala can't seem to make up her mind. She has trouble deciding what to eat or where to go. Kami finds that reciting a rhyme can help her with the process.
Identifiers: LCCN: 2021924706 | ISBN: 978-1-7323906-5-2 (hardcover) | 978-1-7323906-6-9 (paperback) | 978-1-7323906-7-6 (ebook)
Subjects: LCSH Koala--Juvenile fiction. | Decision making--Juvenile fiction. | Children--Life skills guides--Juvenile fiction. | BISAC JUVENILE FICTION / Animals / Zoos | JUVENILE FICTION / Social Themes / Self-Esteem & Self-Reliance | JUVENILE FICTION / Social Themes / General
Classification: LCC PZ7.1.R337 Kam 2022 | DDC [E]--dc23

Dedicated to all the children
who struggle to make decisions.
You are amazing and you can be
the leader of your life!

As soon as Kami Koala opened her eyes, she smelled something yummy.

Kami stopped at the kitchen door. "Oh no," she said.

"I can't decide whether to eat the pancakes or the poached eggs today."

Or maybe I should eat toast instead. It all smells so good."

"Make a decision," Mum said.

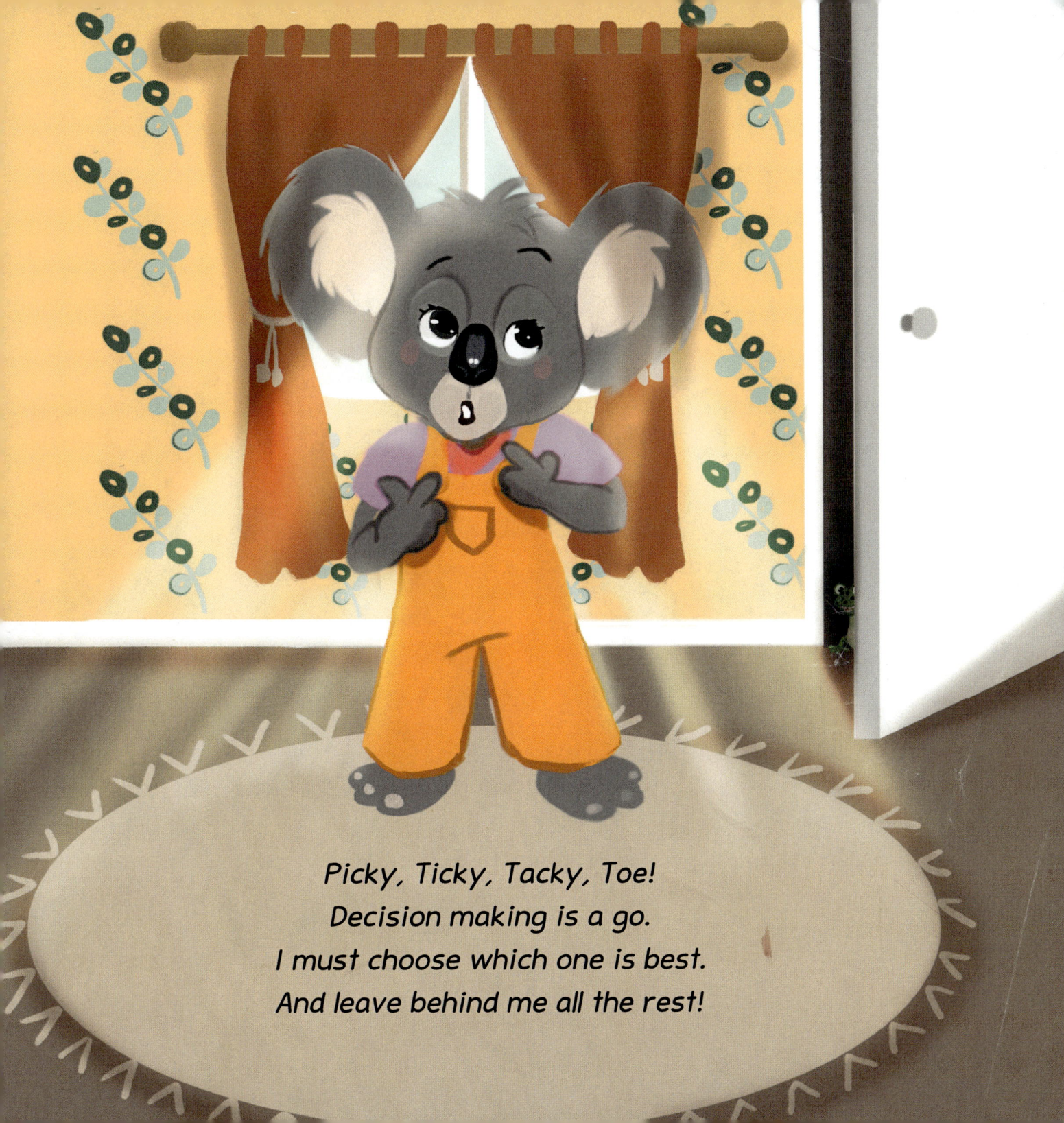

Picky, Ticky, Tacky, Toe!
Decision making is a go.
I must choose which one is best.
And leave behind me all the rest!

"Mum, can you take me to the zoo today?"
Kami asked hopefully.

"Sure," Mum replied. "Sounds like fun!"

"Wait! Maybe we should go to the lake instead. Or the shopping mall. I can't decide."

"Make a decision," Mum said with a smile.
She handed Kami a list of the 3 places:

1. MALL
2. LAKE
3. ZOO

Kami decided to use her favorite decision-making strategy once again.

Kami's finger landed on the zoo.
"Hooray! We're going to the zoo!"
Kami shouted. "I love the zoo–especially the crocodiles!"

1- MALL
2- LAKE
3- ZOO

It wasn't long before she and her mum were in the car, driving to their new adventure.

Mum parked the car and they walked to the zoo entrance. Mum was happy that Kami was able to decide which ticket window to go to.
"I picked the one with the shortest line of people," said Kami. She was proud of her decision.

There were just a few others in line ahead of them, so Kami was patient as they waited their turn.

Standing in line, Kami thought about all the different animals she was about to see. Her excitement was growing.

Kami looked at the map. "What fun!" she said. "There are so many different animals to see— and so many paths to take."

"Mum," Kami said. "I want to see everything and I don't know which animal to see first. I'm not sure if I want to see the elephants first...or the zebras...or the crocodiles."

"Make a decision,"
Mum said.

Once again, Kami Koala decided to use her favorite decision-making strategy.

She sang:

Picky, Ticky, Tacky, Toe!
Decision making is a go.
I must choose which one is best.
And leave behind me all the rest!

"Yay!" Kami shouted. "We're going to see the crocodiles first!"

She held Mum's hand as they followed the map to the crocodiles.

"I think this is what I really wanted all along—eggs for breakfast, a trip to the zoo, and seeing my favorite crocodiles. **I'm good at making decisions!**"

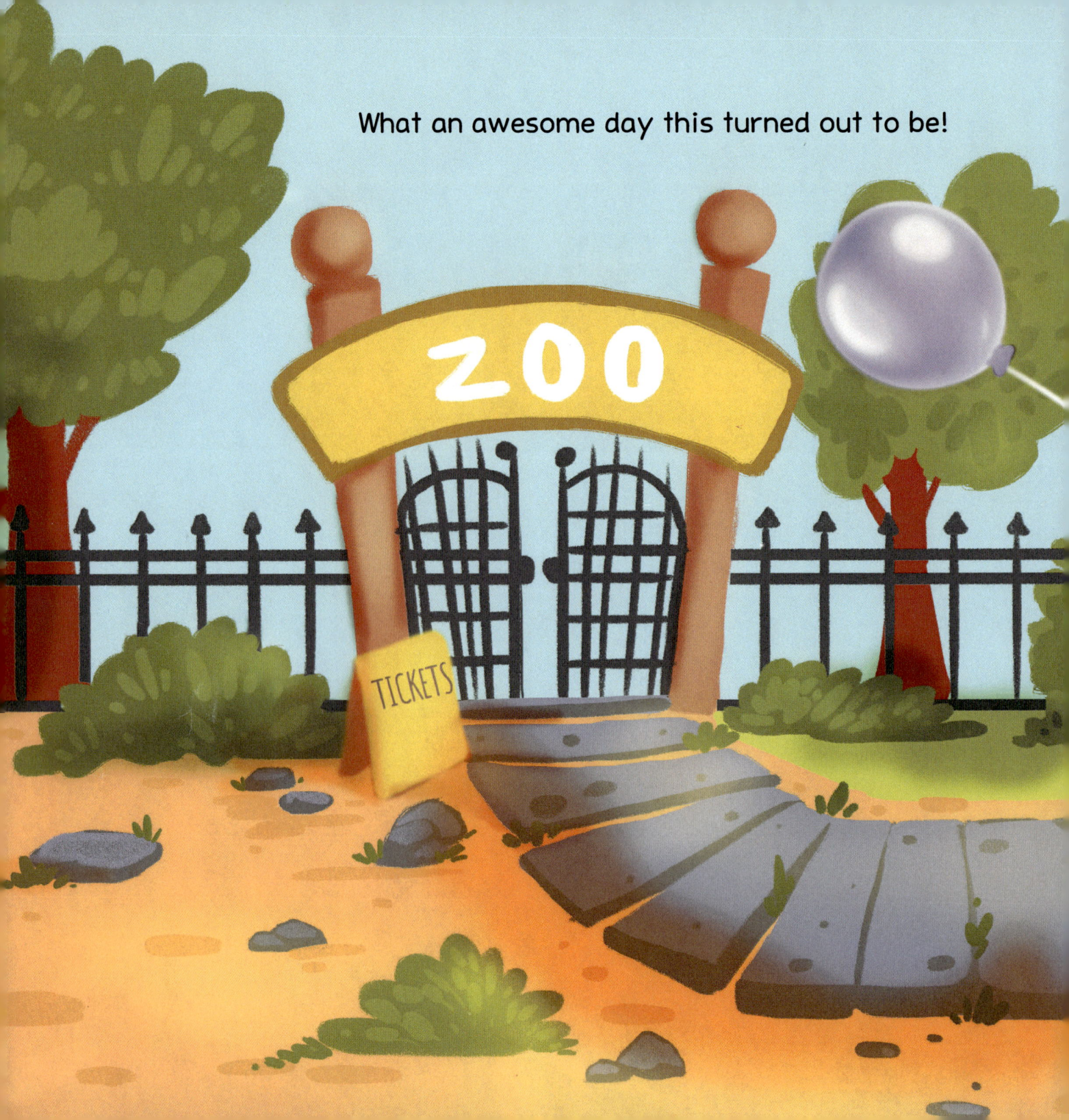
What an awesome day this turned out to be!

Thank you!

I hope your enjoyed reading the book.
There are special downloads waiting for you!
Visit us at www.TeydonRae.com/kami
for decision-making extras including:

Coloring pages, activity pages and more!
We want to know what helps you make good decisions in your life!
Tag us with #KamiKoalaPTTT and you may be featured
on our website and/or social media.

Here is another great book to check out

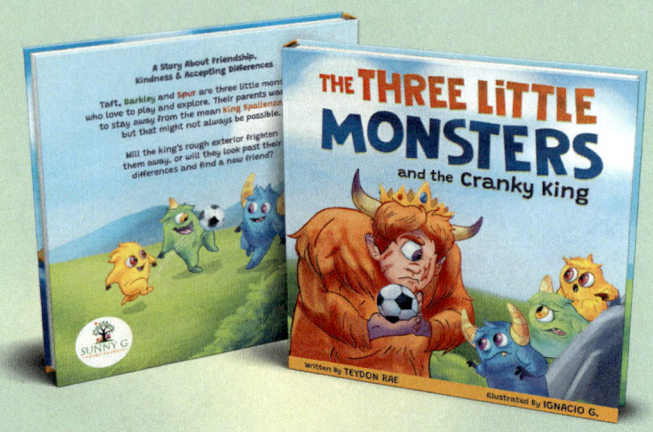

ABOUT THE AUTHOR

Teydon Rae's passion for writing began at a young age. Inspired by an extraordinary teacher whose focus was creativity, she learned to look at the world around her and create fascinating stories, each with an important message.
In addition to pursuing her career as an author, she loves music and literature, and is happy to share her inspiration and creativity with children and families everywhere. Teydon's goal is to inspire creativity in others. She lives in Arizona and enjoy spending time with her husband and children on their family farm.

Made in the USA
Las Vegas, NV
26 November 2022